Antebellum Dream Book

Other Books by Elizabeth Alexander

Body of Life
The Venus Hottentot

Antebellum Dream Book

poems by

Elizabeth Alexander

Graywolf Press
Saint Paul, Minnesota

Publication of this volume is made possible in part by a grant provided by the Minnesota State Arts Board through an appropriation by the Minnesota State Legislature, and by a grant from the National Endowment for the Arts. Significant support has also been provided by the Bush Foundation; Dayton's Project Imagine with support from Target Foundation; the McKnight Foundation; a grant made on behalf of the Stargazer Foundation; and other generous contributions from foundations, corporations, and individuals. To these organizations and individuals we offer our heartfelt thanks.

Published by Graywolf Press
2402 University Avenue, Suite 203
Saint Paul, MN 55114
All rights reserved.

www.graywolfpress.org

Published in the United States of America

ISBN: 1-55597-354-X

2 4 6 8 9 7 5 3 1
First Graywolf Printing, 2001

Library of Congress Control Number: 2001088670

Cover art: Bob Thompson (American, 1937–1966)
  Garden of Music, 1960
  Oil on canvas, 79" × 143"
  Wadsworth Atheneum Museum of Art
  The Ella Gallup Sumner and Mary Catlin Sumner Collection Fund, 1987.4
  Estate of the Artist courtesy Michael Rosenfeld Gallery, NYC.

Cover design: Julie Metz

Acknowledgments

These poems first appeared in the following publications:

The American Voice: "Gravitas"
Boston Review: "Race"
Callaloo: "Orange"
Chicago Review: "Clean," "After the Gig: Mick Jagger"
Crab Orchard Review: "Overture: Watermelon City," "Visitor"
Drumvoices Review: "Georgia Postcard"
Fence: "Untitled," "Hostage"
Hanging Loose: "The Toni Morrison Dreams," "Your Ex-Girlfriend"
Luna: "Elegy," "Early Cinema"
The Massachusetts Review: "Feminist Poem Number One"
Shenandoah: "Fugue"
TriQuarterly: "Neonatology," "'The female seer will burn upon this pyre'"

"Narrative: Ali" appeared in *Every Shut Eye Ain't Asleep: An Anthology of Poetry by African Americans since 1945*, edited by Michael S. Harper and Anthony Walton, published by Little, Brown and Company, 1994, and in *Muhammad Ali: The People's Champ*, edited by Elliot Gorn, published by the University of Illinois Press, 1998.

"Islands Number Four" appeared in *Words for Images: A Gallery of Poems*, edited by John Hollander and Joanna Weber, published by Yale University Art Gallery, 2001

Grateful acknowledgment is made to the editors of these journals and anthologies. The author would also like to thank the Whitney Humanities Center at Yale University, where this manuscript was completed, and the Cave Canem poets' community, which always encouraged the writing of these poems

for Ficre

Contents

I

II

III

I had a dream, its voice spoke to me:
"Why don't you draw or die?"
"Is that it?", I said, "My, My."

Minnie Evans

I

Fugue

1. Walking (1963)

   after the painting by Charles Alston

You tell me, knees are important, you kiss
your elders' knees in utmost reverence.

The knees in this painting are what send the people forward.

Once progress felt real and inevitable,
as sure as the taste of licorice or lemons.
The painting was made after marching
in Birmingham, walking

into a light both brilliant and unseen.

2. 1964

In a beige silk sari
my mother danced the frug
to the Peter Duchin Band.

Earlier that day
at Maison Le Pelch
the French ladies twisted

her magnificent hair
into a fat chignon
while mademoiselle watched,

drank sugared, milky tea,
and counted bobby pins
disappearing in the thick-

ness as the ladies worked
in silence, adornment
so grave, the solemn toilette,

and later, the bath,
and later, red lipstick,
and later, L'Air de Temps.

My mother without glasses.
My mother in beige silk.
My mother with a chignon.
My mother in her youth.

3. 1968

The city burns. We have to stay at home,
TV always interrupted with fire or helicopters.
Men who have tweedled my cheeks once or twice
join the serial dead.

Yesterday I went downtown with Mom.
What a pretty little girl, said the tourists, who were white.
My shoes were patent leather, all shiny, and black.
My father is away saving the world for Negroes,
I wanted to say.

Mostly I go to school or watch television
with my mother and brother, my father often gone.
He makes the world a better place for Negroes.
The year is nineteen-sixty-eight.

4. 1971

"Hey Blood," my father said then
to other brothers in the street.
"Hey, Youngblood, how you doin'?

"Peace and power," he says,
and, "Keep on keepin' on,"
just like Gladys Knight and the Pips.

My stomach jumps: a thrill.
Sometimes poems remember small things, like
"Hey, Blood." My father
still says that sometimes.

5. *The Sun King (1974)*

James Hampton, the Sun King
of Washington, DC
erects a tinfoil throne.
"Where there is no vision, the people perish."
Altar, pulpit, lightbulbs.

My 14th and "U," my 34 bus, my weekday winos,
my white-robed black Israelites
on their redstone stoops,
my graffiti: "Anna the Leo as 'Ice,'"
my neon James Brown poster
coming to the DC Coliseum
where all I will see is the circus,
my one visit to RKO Keith's Theater
to see *Car Wash*
and a bird flew in, and mania,
frantic black shadow on the screen,
I was out of the house in a theater full of black folks,
black people, black movie, black bird,
I was out, I was free, I was at RKO Keith's Theater
at 14th and "U"
and it was not *Car Wash* it was the first
Richard Pryor concert movie
and a bird flew in the screen
and memory is romance,
and race is romance,
and the Sun King lives
in Washington, DC.

Elegy

Motherless, fatherless,
born of no one and everything,

Sun Ra touched down in Birmingham,
The Magic City, city of smokestacks

and tin. He would glitter.
Began departure from Philly,

which is Saturn, in a way.
Said he was no age, never was born.

He's not from no Mars, his sister Mary said.
I peeped through the keyhole. I saw that boy born.

The spaceship left from Birmingham,
city the color of lead, city of trains,

of metal, city of black, black coal.

Overture: Watermelon City

Philadelphia is burning and water-
melon is all that can cool it,
so there they are, spiked
atop a row of metal poles,
rolling on and off pickup trucks,
the fruit that grows longest,
the fruit with a curly tail, the cool fruit,
larger than a large baby, wide
as the widest green behind, wide
vermilion smile at the sizzling metropole.
Did I see this yesterday? Did I dream
this last night? The city is burning,
is burning for real.

When I first moved here I lived two streets over
from Osage, where it happened, twelve streets down.
I asked my neighbors, who described
the smell of smoke and flesh,
the city on fire for real.
How far could you see the flames?
How long could you smell the smoke?
Osage is narrow, narrow
like a movie set: urban eastern seaboard,
the tidy of people who work hard for very little.

Life lived on the porch,
the amphitheater street.
I live here, 4937 Hazel Avenue, West Philly.
Hello, Adam and Ukee,
the boys on that block
who guarded my car, and me.
They called him Ukee because

as a baby he looked
like a eucalyptus leaf.
Hello, holy rollers
who plug in their amps,
blow out the power in the building,
preach to the street from the stoop.
Hello, crack-head next-door neighbor
who raps on my door after midnight
needing money for baby formula,
she says, and the woman
who runs in the street
with her titties out, wailing.
Hello, street. Hello, ladies
who sweep their front porches each morning.
In downtown Philadelphia
there are many lovely restaurants,
reasonably priced.
Chocolate, lemon ice,
and hand-filled cannolis
in South Philly.
Around the corner
at the New Africa Lounge
in West Philadelphia
we sweat buckets
to hi-life and zouk,
we burn.

Early Cinema

According to Mister Hedges, the custodian
who called upon their parents
after young Otwiner and young Julia
were spotted at the matinee
of Rudolph Valentino in *The Sheik*
at the segregated Knickerbocker Theater
in the uncommon Washington December
of 1922, "Your young ladies
were misrepresenting themselves today,"
meaning, of course, that they were passing.
After coffee and no cake were finished
and Mister Hedges had buttoned his coat
against the strange evening chill,
choice words were had with Otwiner and Julia,
shame upon the family, shame upon the race.

How they'd longed to see Rudolph Valentino,
who was swarthy like a Negro, like the finest Negro man.
In *The Sheik*, they'd heard, he was turbaned,
whisked damsels away in a desert cloud.
They'd heard this from Lucille and Ella
who'd put on their fine frocks and French,
claiming to be "of foreign extraction"
to sneak into the Knickerbocker Theater
past the usher who knew their parents
but did not know them.
They'd heard this from Mignon and Doris
who'd painted carmine bindis on their foreheads
braided their black hair tight down the back,
and huffed, "We'll have to take this up with the Embassy"
to the squinting ticket taker.
Otwiner and Julia were tired of Oscar Michaux,

tired of church, tired of responsibility,
rectitude, posture, grooming, modulation,
tired of homilies each way they turned,
tired of colored right and wrong.
They wanted to be whisked away.

The morning after Mister Hedges' visit
the paperboy cried "Extra!" and Papas
shrugged camel's hair topcoats over pressed pajamas,
and Mamas read aloud at the breakfast table,
"No Colored Killed When Roof Caves In"
at the Knickerbocker Theater
at the evening show
from a surfeit of snow on the roof.
One hundred others dead.

It appeared that God had spoken.
There was no school that day,
no movies for months after.

Paul Says

White people need to get a life,
need to feed the world instead of cloning sheep
and dreaming how to make more of themselves.

Paul says his father used to tell him
what to tell the other black kids at school
who told him he talked like a white boy.
"Well, you talk like a white boy, too.
The only difference is, you talk like an ignorant,
uneducated white boy." When he hears teenagers
yelling in the street, he says, if my kids talk like that,
I'm sending their asses to Switzerland.

Paul says his sister used to go out with an African,
a Nigerian. "When she wouldn't give up the pussy,
he locked her in the apartment, and she had to use jujitsu
to escape, so you'd better be careful." Paul says Washington, DC
is better for the skin than Chicago, that his sister was born
with hair down to her waist and a full set of teeth.

When I was little, Paul said, I wanted to be a herpetologist,
so my father bought me snakes. Oakland in my childhood
was magical. Afros everywhere. I used to have a butterfly net.

Hosea Williams

(1926—2000)

Rabble-rousing lunchbreaks
in his white chemist's coat.

Some NAACP-types
cared his parents never wed.

Clubs, dogs, the Edmund Pettus Bridge,
drop and pray, they keep on coming.

Curses which look to be prayer.
Red shirt, bib overalls, sneakers.

My wild man! My Castro!
King called him.

My blind mother,
blind broom-making father,

what I do for them,
what they did for me.

Nineteen-sixty-three: still
as a swamp, as a goldfish

swimming in a cut-glass bowl.

Georgia Postcard

I. Atlanta

The black men
are fine
and abundant
at the airport.
The women
have spent
many hours
on their hair.

II. Sixty-Five MPH

All-u-can eat,
boiled shrimp, fried fish.

Highway Church of God:
"You come in here and pray."

Roadkill, and blackbirds
that pick at it,

chain gangs, and fat scarlet clover
in rippling flocks—

a North Georgia spring,
a spreading rash, blush.

III. Kin: Sparta, Georgia

106-year-old
Great-Aunt Kate

calls it "the dry grin,"
what white people give you
when they want you to think
you are safe
when you're not.

IIII. Green

How you would love
the pale green trees,
the sheer chartreuse light,
the swallowing kudzu,
the mammoth dogwoods,
the Christmas tree farm.

Visitor

Belo Horizonte

The city rocks at close of day,
buses lumber, workers hustle home.
Sunlight's a silt on these buildings
outside my hotel window. I am high up,
a visitor to this new city, excited
and weary as Lorca or Senghor. Here,
they say it straight: white women
to marry, black women for work,
mulattas for fucking. There are hundreds
of words describing color, skin, and who
I would be in this city is unclear.

A car horn plays "La Cucaracha,"
just like Uptown, USA. Streetlights
and headlights appear like chicken pox.
I could look out this window for hours
at the finishing day, the lancets
and whippets of shiny rose light.
My eyes are a gemologist's, divining
mica from mud, mining iridescence,
a country, composed in legible lumens, color.

Days later on the night-flight,
almost West and home, the wide sky wakes.
America becomes visible beneath plush clouds
outside bituminous Pittsburgh,
gray and mottled, gridless, dappled.

Then the clouds clot and we are in heaven.

I am black again. The sky is pale and pink.

My suitcase is full of poems in Portuguese,
beads to protect me that will break in a month,
vacuum-packed coffee beans, ebony fists,
black soap that lathers up creamy, and white.

Geraniums

In my front yard, Negro
flower,

"When Sue Wears Red," Negro
genius behind a picket fence,

nodding heads, blooms
smell spice, not sweet,

burred green splinters,
common weed, edible green—

geraniums in my front yard,
survivors, nigger red.

Islands Number Four

1.

Agnes Martin, *Islands Number Four,*
Repeated ovals on a grid, what appears
To be perfect is handmade, disturbed.
Tobacco brown saturates canvas to burlap,
Clean form from a distance, up close, her hand.
All wrack and bramble to oval and grid.
Hollows in the body, containers for grief.
What looks to be perfect is not perfect.

Odd oval portholes that flood with light.

2.

Description of a Slave Ship, 1789:
Same imperfect ovals, calligraphic hand.
At a distance, pattern. Up close, bodies
Doubled and doubled, serried and stacked
In the manner of galleries in a church,
In full ships on their sides or on each other.
Isle of woe, two-by-two, spoon-fashion,
Not unfrequently found dead in the morning.
Slave ships, the not pure, imperfect ovals,
Portholes through which they would never see home,
The flesh rubbed off their shoulders, elbows, hips.
Barracoon, sarcophagus, indestructible grief
Nesting in the hollows of the abdomen.
The slave ship empty, its cargo landed
And sold for twelve ounces of gold apiece

Or gone overboard. Islands. Aftermath.

Nat Turner Dreams of Insurrection

... too much sense to be raised, and if I was,
I would never be of any service to any one as a slave.

The Confessions of Nat Turner, 1831

Drops of blood on the corn, as dew from heaven.
Forms of men in different attitudes, portrayed in blood.
Numbers, glyphs, on woodland leaves, also in blood.

Freedom: a dipperful of cold well water.
Freedom: the wide white sky.
Dreams that make me sweat.

Because I am called, I must appear so, prepare.
I am not a conjurer. Certain marks on my head and breast.
Shelter me, Great Dismal Swamp. A green-blue sky which roils.

Race

Sometimes I think about Great-Uncle Paul who left Tuskegee,
Alabama to become a forester in Oregon and in so doing
became fundamentally white for the rest of his life, except
when he traveled without his white wife to visit his siblings—
now in New York, now in Harlem, USA—just as pale-skinned,
as straight-haired, as blue-eyed as Paul, and black. Paul never told anyone
he was white, he just didn't say that he was black, and who could imagine,
an Oregon forester in 1930 as anything other than white?
The siblings in Harlem each morning ensured
no one confused them for anything other than what they were, black.
They were black! Brown-skinned spouses reduced confusion.
Many others have told, and not told, this tale.
When Paul came East alone he was as they were, their brother.

The poet invents heroic moments where the pale black ancestor stands up
on behalf of the race. The poet imagines Great-Uncle Paul
in cool, sagey groves counting rings in redwood trunks,
imagines pencil markings in a ledger book, classifications,
imagines a sidelong look from an ivory spouse who is learning
her husband's caesuras. She can see silent spaces
but not what they signify, graphite markings in a forester's code.

Many others have told, and not told, this tale.
The one time Great-Uncle Paul brought his wife to New York
he asked his siblings not to bring their spouses,
and that is where the story ends: ivory siblings who would not
see their brother without their telltale spouses.
What a strange thing is "race," and family, stranger still.
Here a poem tells a story, a story about race.

II

Gravitas

Emergency! A bright yellow school bus
is speeding me to hospital. My pregnant belly bulges
beneath my pleated skirt, the face
of my dear niece Amal a locket inside my stomach.

Soon she will be born healthy,
and after, her sister, Bana.
Labor will be tidy and effortless.
In fact, I will hardly remember it!

All of this is taking place in Kenya, where they live.
This is my first dream of pregnancy
since I have been actually pregnant,
therefore I dream in reality rather than metaphor.

I am gravid, eight weeks along.
My baby, I have read, has a tail
and a spine made of pearls,
and every day I speak to her in tongues.

Baby

The doctor handed me a parfait dish
of melting pink and coffee ice cream
and said, "Congratulations! A girl!"
This bewildered me; I had not been
pregnant, but I kissed the dish and put her
in the deep freeze to see if she'd take shape.
I knew there was a baby in there somewhere,
her tiny arms and legs in vaguest outline.
The doctor frowned, then smiled again:
"Congratulations! A boy!" This one
had a mammoth head and a full set
of teeth. I named the babies Vincent and Louise.
Meanwhile, my father fluttered about
the room and discouraged visitors.
My mother-in-law said, "I made you turkey
breast and rice. You didn't eat." My husband
slept deeply on my brother's bunk bed.
I talked about the dream and later thought
about something someone told me, that
giving birth is all about yourself.
I am formless and fanged, boy and girl both,
food and baby at the very same time.

Lament

We argue. I dream we live where I used to live
with the man I used to love who stands
outside the building throwing snowballs,
his belongings scattered on the sidewalk
because I have evicted him. He knows
the ins and outs of this apartment, could
easily enter, like a mouse with a flexible spine
sliding beneath a closed door.

I struggle to understand arguments,
their epistemologies. One argument
can't burn the pot to crust, can't tarnish everything.
I keep tasting the word "Armageddon," remember
a government job long ago where office mates
showed lunch-hour films on the imminent end of the world,
Jesus Christ as the only antidote.

                        There is no Christ
in this dream, no frogs or fishes, no white light,
just snowballs pelted at the window of the home
I share with one I have pledged to love forever, the windows
gaping open, the word "Armageddon" hard and icy in my mouth.

Crash

I am the last woman off of the plane
that has crashed in a cornfield near Philly,

picking through hot metal
for my rucksack and diaper bag.

No black box, no fuselage,
just sistergirl pilot wiping soot from her eyes,

happy to be alive. Her dreadlocks
will hold the smoke for weeks.

All the white passengers bailed out
before impact, so certain a sister

couldn't navigate the crash. O gender.
O race. O ye of little faith.

Here we are in the cornfield, bruised and dirty but alive.
I invite sistergirl pilot home for dinner

at my parents', for my mother's roast chicken
with gravy and rice, to celebrate.

Nat King Cole on the Amalfi Drive

He sings after making the beast with two backs,
something low-down and dirty, fried liver and onions,
put your hands on your hips and let your diction slip.

We do it real quick. I am "that kind of girl."
He shakes out his marcel, calls Yes!
to the Lord, caretaker of bliss, maker of figs,

the good Lord of smothered chicken and biscuits
who gave us five senses, said, Go forth and taste
for your time on this earth is not long.

We keep our pleasure secret, dahlias
underneath my skirt as I watch from the studio audience.
The Negro crooner sings of "Eskeemos."

Wild applause from the flush-cheeked fans.
My dahlias rustle, brush. A wink for me,
a smile for me, for me in black and white.

The Toni Morrison Dreams

1.

Toni Morrison despises
conference coffee, so I offer
to fetch her a Starbucks
macchiato grande, with turbinado sugar.

She's delighted, can start her day properly,
draws on her Gauloises,
shakes her gorgeous, pewter dreads,
sips the java that I brought her
and reads her own words:

> *Nuns go by as quiet as lust*

Everything in silver-gray and black.

2. Workshop

She asks us to adapt
Synge's *Playboy of the Western World*
for the contemporary stage.
She asks us to translate "The Birds."

She asks us to think about clocks,
see the numbers as glyphs,
consider the time we spend watching them

in class, on line, at the hairdresser's.

In class she calls me "Ouidah" and I answer.

"I am the yellow mother
of two yellow boys," she says.
I sit up straight.

Now the work begins, and
Oh
the work is hard.

3.

She does not love
my work, but she loves

my baby, tells me
to have many more.

4. A Reading at Temple University

"Love," she wrote,
and "love" and "love" and "love,"

and "amanuensis," "velvet," "pantry," "lean,"

Shadrack, Solomon, Hagar, Jadine, Plum,

circles   sth   runagate

and then,
she whispered it,

love

"The female seer will burn upon this pyre"

Sylvia Plath is setting my hair
on rollers made from orange-juice cans.
The hairdo is shaped like a pyre.

My locks are improbably long.
A pyramid of lemons somehow
balances on the rickety table

where we sit, in the rented kitchen
which smells of singed naps and bergamot.
Sylvia Plath is surprisingly adept

at rolling my unruly hair.
She knows to pull it tight.
                              Few words.
Her flat, American belly,

her breasts in a twin sweater set,
stack of typed poems on her desk,
envelopes stamped to go by the door,

a freshly baked poppyseed cake,
kitchen safety matches, black-eyed Susans
in a cobalt jelly jar. She speaks a word,

"immolate," then a single sentence
of prophecy. The hairdo done,
the nursery tidy, the floor swept clean

of burnt hair and bumblebee husks.

War

In the dream there was goo,
yellow goo which hurled itself
at unclothed bodies, and burned.
Shower water slowing to a trickle,
mayhem on TV and on the radio.

Dan Rather in slow motion:
We thought they'd attack
a medium-sized city of poor people,
like Philadelphia,
not a mighty city like Chicago.

Tanks, firing with no sound.
Mayhem, a word I've been drawn to
for the last week for no apparent reason,
my newest, pulsing word
in a dream where I do not picture enemies.

Hostage

As far as we can
determine they have been
unharmed.

Heads will roll, motherfuckers.
I'll chop 'em off.
I'll throw 'em in the street.

Taxicab, monkey mask, black lace brassiere,
condom, alligator, Seminole Indian,

the Western Hemisphere,

geranium, flowerpot, Oyster School,
coconut bra, unmarked vehicle, stretch limousine.

I am from DC,
therefore responsible.
I am terrified of heights.

Exciting things like this never happen to me.

Tour Guide

You have discovered Indian cliff dwellings
at the Kennedy compound in Hyannis Port
and are clambering where the signs say "no,"
disrupting the tour, snapping photographs,
asking loud questions about how and where
the Indians lived as the tour guide insists
only Kennedys ever lived there. I see the rock paintings
clear as day, on the seaside crags where you point to them.

We're asked to leave, but you have gathered evidence:
infrared pictures of glyphs, cave windows, arrowheads.
As we leave the tour guides give us armfuls
of Cuban cigars: Here are your relics, your artifacts,
the objects of people who lived here and disappeared.

But we know who was here first. We have photographs.

Untitled

If you win a MacArthur genius grant
they bring you to a meeting in New York.
Wear casual clothes, shirtsleeves, dungarees.

The lot of you sit around a table
and the leader asks you what your thinking looks like,
literally, what does your thinking look like?

My thinking is drenched with light,
as something dusted with pollen, sheer like that.

My thinking is a series of crosshatches
with holes like an old screen window
and the holes keep getting bigger.

My thinking looks like blue vapor,
red sparks, yellow tildes, then viscosity.

My thinking is a wet, glazed thing which glitters.

Very good, says the leader, like school, when we finish.
She gives each of us a treat, a hush puppy
formed in the shape of a fish, a small fish,
smaller than a porgy, bigger than a smelt.
They are golden-brown and crisp
like a simple, well-executed thought.

Clean

Dreamt of almost-viscous water
coming up the bathtub drain.
I cannot mop it clean.

*Clorinda, the Girl Who Slipped
Down the Drain* is a book
from my mother's childhood.

Through the drain and the pipes
she found lilies and frogs,
English-speaking amphibians, no crocodiles.

Once I saw a baby alligator
frozen, mid-crawl, emerging
from the gutter in Chicago

where lake waves freeze
mid-crest in the winter
and water beneath is gelatinous.

Dreamt I shat a bar
of Lever Brothers soap,
a huge white lovely cake,

and then my stomach shrank
and shrank and shrank and shrank
until it had nothing inside.

Guten Tag, Dr. Freud!
Bonjour, Claude Levi-Strauss!
At last, I am totally clean!

Peccant

Maryland State Correctional Facility for Women,
Baltimore County Branch, has undergone a face-lift.
Cells are white and ungraffitied, roomlike, surprisingly airy.
This is where I must spend the next year, eating slop from tin trays,
facing women much tougher than I am, finding out if I am brave.
Though I do not know what I took, I know I took something.

On Exercise Day, walk the streets of the city you grew up in,
in my case, DC, from pillar to post, Adams-Morgan to Anacostia,
Shaw to Southwest, Logan to Chevy Chase Circles,
recalling every misbegotten everything, lamenting, repenting.

How my parents keen and weep, scheme to spring me,
intercept me at corners with bus tokens, pass keys, files baked in cakes.
Komunyakaa the poet says, don't write what you know,
write what you are willing to discover, so I will
spend this year, these long days, meditating on what I am accused of
in the white rooms, city streets, communal showers, mess hall,
where all around me sin and not sin is scraped off tin trays
into oversized sinks, all that excess, scraped off and rinsed away.

Papi Lindo vs The Beautiful Man

The beautiful one is the ultimate victor
in this dream, you, who stand before me
in the dream damp from the shower and smiling,
in a fresh white suit which has gardenias
for buttons down the front. You are framed
in a doorway; the dream is a black and white movie.
I beam at your beauty, the flowers, but tell you,
I don't want Papi Lindo, so you pluck
off the gardenias one by one and hand them
all to me; I gorge on their sick white sweet-
ness, and there you are before me, in a plain
white suit with no buttons, a beautiful man.

Saber-Toothed

What a fabulous living room!
the guests are exclaiming,
Just like my parents' from the '70s!
Parquet floors, beanbag chairs,
port-fenêtre onto the bricked patio,
a sunken conversation pit.

Here is the Roto-Rooter woman
with her giant orange snake, come to clear out the drain.
A saber-toothed tiger leaps out
of the manhole in the living room
and swallows a guest from head to toe!
He aims straight for me but I grab one saber tooth
and he slinks back down the drain.

I have dreamed of dalmations in my bedroom,
alligators in my bathroom, rodents
too numerous to count. Always
the house is collapsing, the plaster crumbling,
architecture disappearing all around me.

The manhole is my only permeable aperture today.
At least I can seal it tight.

Today I am empress of the living room,
queen of my house, no tiger,
no squirrel, no cockroach, no mouse.

Conch Chowder

"I'm making conch chowder," says my next-door neighbor, Joe. There are no walls between our apartments. "We'll all watch basketball," he says, "and we'll eat it with French bread." I tell him that I have to run an errand.

Next thing I know, I'm outside New York, looking for a roadside Holocaust museum I'd read about, I had to see. I find it, hand-lettered signs, an old woman on a bench with a heavy Polish accent. A young man and his son go inside; you go down into the Invisible Man's basement, which is wildly lit up and makeshift, and you look out at the world from that small space. I begin to cry. I cry and cry and cry. Then it's time to go home, so I look for a cab. How much would it cost to go from Jersey to Chicago?

Everyone is upset when I get there. Danielle, Joe's wife, says we have to have a family meeting, no more lateness, no more unexplained absences. My eyes fill up again when she says the word, "family." I sit down in front of the TV and eat my conch chowder, which is cold.

Pig

Held a whole baby pig
in my mouth, halfway
down my throat, waiting
for word if I should swallow
because it was my dinner.

Rollerblade, Inc.

Ex-husband arrives on Rollerblades
while I am in the kitchen making caramel.
The white sugar melts, turns brown, then burns.

Do I add water? Do I add milk?
The ex-husband skates figure eights
on the hardwood floor in the living room

and I am taking care not to burn myself
on the handle of the cast-iron skillet
or the brown lacquer sheet of scorched sugar.

He doesn't speak, he just skates, then leaves.
I think: he didn't close the door behind him.
I think: I have burned my caramel.

I think: Rollerblade, Inc. A trade name.

The Creole Cat

I am in New Orleans with my two friends Jennifer and Anna, and with George C. Wolfe, who I do not know in real life but feel I will someday know. We are in a bordello, watching the show and drinking Sazeracs, which are bright green in this dream. I leave in the middle of "La Ramona" and cross the tracks to a maze of streets where everyone is shooting drugs and fucking. Luckily, I can run a few steps and then fly, so I do, and return to my friends. Jennifer has changed into costume. She is more fabulous than Eartha Kitt or Josephine, in a black, crushed-velvet leotard, bugle beads at the hips, opera-length, poison-green gloves, a black cat mask. She dances like curly seaweed, and in a French accent she sings, "I am the original Creole Cat, the first black woman to play this role. I don't have to perform my blackness. I inhabit it." George C. Wolfe is thrilled, says he'll put her on the main stage at the Joe Papp Public Theater. He'll make her a star.

Opiate

A date with Michael Jordan proves
he is a true gentleman, arrives smiling,
bearing a bouquet of red carnations,
driving a modest sports car, in a sober
but stylish navy-blue suit. He grins that grin.
Hello Michael Jordan then off you go,
have your date, then have lovely safe sex,
after which you remember, you are married,
you don't know Michael Jordan, even though
he is your age-mate, and lumbers
off the championship court nowadays
looking much like you do after nursing
your newborn at four in the morning
blue night after inky blue night.

"Michael Jordan
is the opiate of the masses," comes a voice
at the end of the dream, perhaps John Cameron Swayze
or James Earl Jones as Darth Vader. "Michael Jordan
is the opiate of the masses." Opiates are verboten
for nursing moms like me. Improbable, ominous;
our date was so *Father Knows Best,* so
Mayberry RFD, such a wide, wide grin.
I wake to a foghorn, "Opiate of the masses,"

no memory of the feel of his dark and lovely skin.

Movie Star

In the dream, I slept with Jack Nicholson.
I snuck away from home and had to lie about my whereabouts,
said I was sleeping at Nicole's when really I was sleeping with Jack
    Nicholson.

Cut to a parking lot, a gray and stormy day.
Mom and Dad and Mark and I have just been to the movies.
Dad and I take one car, Mom and Mark, the other.

Jack Nicholson gives great presents if you sleep with him.
He gave me a bathroom caddy filled with every cosmetic I love:

aspirins and lotions and potpourri perfume, fifteen different shades of
    brown lipstick, a boar-bristle brush, Florida water, pimple cream.

Receta Culinaria

Make soup from this:

Shrimp shells for stock,
yams, mushrooms (portobello),
cilantro to taste.

Tomato

My friend Amy has a jones for pregnant women,
wants to fan their flushed faces, pull out chairs for them,
carry parasols above them in strong sunlight,
fix figs with mascarpone for the calcium and iron.

I long to be the rosy, pregnant woman people flock to,
hear other women's chuttering wisdom, tales:
a sister whose teeth fell out from too many babies,
milk that spurts across the room at any cry.
Her hair went curly. Her hair went straight.
Her face erupted in red sprinkles.
How are you eating? What are you dreaming?
Dream of strawberries, the baby will have rashes.

And then one night I dream of Susan Sarandon.
She's a radiant red tomato in a straw sun hat,
digging in the rows of her organic garden patch,
a million months pregnant,

and her lover is feeding her chocolate, square by square.

After the Gig: Mick Jagger

The baby cries. Mick Jagger swaggers backstage,
lit with sweat. The crowd still screams outside.
He's been second-lining with a gaggle of New Orleans Negroes,
a white parasol, wears toreador pants and is bare-chested, bones.

I've forgiven the Rolling Stones for fetishizing me
and my sisters in "Brown Sugar" and "Some Girls."
Black girls, black girls, black girls.   *unimportant stuff*
Why does so much flotsam populate my brain?
Why not ancient Ge'ez, the Mingus discography,

suminagashi paper technique,

something utilitarian?

This is a four weeks postpartum dream. Mick Jagger's
black baby cries again. Thank God, it isn't mine.
Gotta go, love, gotta go, he says,
and shrugs his bony shoulders,
grins that reptile-mammal grin,

picks the baby up, coo-coos,

and then rocks that baby down.

Postpartum Dream #2: Folk Art

It's me! Discovered in a sleeve
of cellulose negatives

in a fusty gray basement
at the Archive of Afro-American Art

amidst fading Tanners
and lost Douglas diptychs,

Fon masks and walking sticks, baptismal fonts,
dream quilts of meteor showers,

a Bob Thompson Cirque du Soleil—
and me! At three,

in a scarlet snowsuit, next to Mother
holding Brother on her hip.

Then I am my mother, Metrecal-slim,
a Catlett madonna. Astonishment. Mama!

Basement walls suddenly Bill Traylor blue.

Postpartum Dream #8

In a hail of bazooka fire they drop
her toddler from the second-floor porch.
She knows he'll land in bushes and survive.
They'll leave him for dead. When the shots subside
she'll grab him, shush him, shrink him pocket-sized,
kung-fu fight to the basement crawl space
to plan how to rescue the six-week-old baby.
The toddler thinks she's the mother in all his books,
Mama Tiger, Mama Bear, Mama Elephant: "Mama."
What else is she to do with all that pride?

Look right, look left. She runs head-down, toddler
in her pocket, straight to Foster Care, where
she sweeps away paperwork, storms marble corridors,
high heels clicking past uniformed matrons
and rows of bassinets 'til she sees
the silver arc of her sweet baby's pee.
Baby! My baby! His mouth at the ready,
her nipples stand out from here to St. Louis,
unsexy and mighty, full of that much milk.

Postpartum Dream #12: Appointment

I answered all
the Chief Justice's questions
impeccably, and it wasn't
very hard.

I waited
with my father
for the phone call.

"I guess I'll be
the first black woman
on the Supreme Court
if I get this."

"Damn straight,"
said my dad.

The President
appeared on television
playing golf and smiling.
He has a secret.
His secretary phones
and asks the question.

Maybe I could do it
when the baby
goes to kindergarten. Maybe
I could do it
on alternate Mondays.
Maybe my baby
could gurgle and coo
in a pen in my chambers,

pulling at the curls
on my barrister's wig,
spitting up on my black robes.

Meanwhile,

I'm excited. I turned out
to be a good lawyer, the best,

just like my dad.

Evidence

Like everyone else, I dream I've been raped long ago and forgotten it, by a boy I knew from eighth grade, the sweetest boy at school. How could I have forgotten, I ask myself, and it's not until I go back and get school records that say I spent months in the infirmary with "a bleeding vagina" I believe that it must have been true.

The rapist is coming back to get me because I have remembered. He knows too much about me, when I leave my house and walk along the lake, when I go to sleep, where the wires in my house are. I try to wake my lover and tell him, The rapist is near! The bedside light flickers and I hear him in the room! The rapist has turned into Arsenio Hall. Later, I think about that name. Arsenio, arsenic, arsenal, arsonist, a name which is closest to "fire."

The Party

Obi had a big ole party
for his birthday, in New York City,
with an African band called Difunkt.

Harry Belafonte came,
sang "Rum and Coconut Water."
We ate while we rocked to the beat.

You had to dress in costume,
so I came as Nefertiti,
with sandals laced up my ankles

and a papier-mâché crown.
Floating in a pan of water
was a hydroponic baobab tree,

free-floating, without any roots.
The baby inside of me danced,
and thumped so hard my Nefertiti

dress blew up all around me!
And we floated eggs in the water.
At the end of a baobab's life

their trunks explode into water!
Explode, explode, explode,
and the baby inside of me danced.

Orange

The doctor has diagnosed cancer, sees
"shadows" and "masses" in the sad, damp bags
which are my lungs. I have three weeks at best.

I am running through Idlewild airport, wheezing,
as I race to catch the evening flight to Paris.
I want to be bumped up to first class, I have cancer,
want champagne, toasted nuts and extra legroom,
crave comfort, however it comes.

                              Miss one train,
catch another, said a friend's wise mother,
meaning, keep on keeping on, meaning
get back on the horse, meaning it ain't over
'til it's over, 'til the fat lady sings.
Can the baby now quickening inside me
survive on its own? I'd asked the doctor.
This was my first thought, my first such thought.
Yes, he'd reassured me, she'll be tiny,
but babies, like cancers, grow and grow.

I can't run fast enough. I miss that plane.
A man dressed all in orange whisks me
to his mother's, shows his first-edition books,
autobiographies, of Angela Davis, Joe Louis,
Muhammad Ali. Then he lifts his mother's mattress,
displays a million dollars in small bills.
He tells me wise things, wise things I can't remember
but take in like mentholated steam:

I'm dead,

he said, I died at 37. It's not so bad.
I come back when I need to, walk amongst you
leaving signs that I passed through. The dead
wear orange when they come back to visit.
That is how you know which ones we are.

Life as Dinner Party

Tonight is a dinner party gone awry.
First, there is not enough food.
I've purchased rotisserie chicken for four,
made a salad with gorgonzola dressing
but the company keeps coming!
My students, invited for *Friday,*
arrive *Thursday,* dressed to kill,
bearing street-vendor iris and gold chocolate boxes.
They take up all the chairs I have
and dig into my chicken.
Then my parents arrive with my brother's children
and strange uncles I've never met
who wear yellow suits and drive late-model Cadillacs.
One brings a Smithfield ham, grins spaciously,
tells me with a wink that it's presliced.
Then Amy Cappellazzo calls, Amy,
big bad Italian girl, ex-object of my affections.
Ciao bella, she says. Who's there and who's fabulous?
and she's on her way, bringing peppercorn pâté.

Here is my motley life at this mismatched dinner table.
Mike Tyson's on TV and George Foreman knocks him out.
Kayo! shout the yellow-suited uncles.
But somehow, there is plenty to eat. We find more chairs.
La Donna Cappellazzo arrives looking smashing,
chattering into her tiny cell phone.
And finally, finally, you come, as you always do,
bearing coconut sorbet packed in tiny coco shells
enough for everyone, extra for me,
so cool, so pure, so white, so sweet.

Visitation

Pablo Neruda still lives in my dream,
will discuss with me a better language
for poems both "political" and "personal,"
dandles my poppy-faced baby on his knee,
offers to blurb my latest collection,
prefers English to Spanish this bright afternoon
(but oh how my Spanish glitters in this dream!).
I remember to him his great poems, muses:
Matilde Urrutia, "Amores: Josie Bliss," "Walking Around,"
lines that made the words inside me shift and organize.
He understands why I fall asleep sometimes
when Important Visitors lecture at the University.
Of course you fall asleep, he says, and waves.
Adios, cariña. You're off to write a poem.

Feminist Poem Number One

Yes I have dreams where I am rescued by men:
my father, brother, husband, no one else.
Last night I dreamed my brother and husband
morphed into each other and rescued me
from a rat-infested apartment. "Run!"
he said, feral scampering at our heels.
And then we went to lunch at the Four Seasons.

What does it mean to be a princess?
"I am what is known as an American Negro,"
my grandmother would say, when "international friends"
would ask her what she was. She'd roller-skate
to Embassy Row and sit on the steps of the embassies
to be certain the rest of the world was there.

What does it mean to be a princess?
My husband drives me at 6 A.M.
to the airport an hour away, drives home,
drives back when I have forgotten my passport.
What does it mean to be a prince? I cook
savory, fragrant meals for my husband
and serve him, if he likes, in front of the TV.
He cooks for me, too. I have a husband.

In the dream we run into Aunt Lucy,
who is waiting for a plane from "Abyssinia"
to bring her lover home. I am the one
married to an Abyssinian, who is already here. I am the one
with the grandmother who wanted to know the world.
I am what is known as an American Negro princess,

married to an African prince,
living in a rat-free apartment in New Haven,
all of it, all of it, under one roof.

Your Ex-Girlfriend

Is hollering from her New York tenement window,
throwing keys from the fifth floor down to the man
she picked up at a discotheque last night.
His arms are full of gifts wrapped in pink paper,
her hair is long and mangy, hangs almost to the street.
Your sisters say she was a tramp, but you say
you can't see it, her smile tells all the truth.

In a nearby rehearsal hall I am busy
learning the dances from *West Side Story*.
I can't keep my stockings from running, or from bagging
at the knees. When we take five, I eat vegetable soup
with Aunt Maggie, who was a dance-hall gypsy back in the day.
We sit in the sun and I tell her why I love you.
The phrase most repeated is "capacity for joy."

Then you appear and we take the freight elevator up.
The ex-girlfriend has showered, and cut her stringy hair.
Her arms are full of joy: *The Joy of Cooking, Joy of Sex,*
Joy dishwashing liquid, Joy perfume by Jean Patou.
Joy is so important, your ex-girlfriend says, and smiles.
You've got to keep your life absolutely full of it.

Gift

I dreamed I forgot to say thank you
to someone who gave me a gift.

Amphibious cheekbones and brow, tobacco skin,
white carnation bath, white light in the water.
Then I was clean, and lit out for the territory,

Chicago on a bicycle, splendid metropolis, ghetto heaven,
Humboldt Park, chiquitas, white summer dresses,
vendor alcapurrias, front porch, chicken in the kitchen,
lunch break, back to the Lake,
heal a sad soul in her exhausted body.

He took the pan from me and finished cooking, said, Rest.
Like a man he would disappear—
(An ugly part which does not bear retelling.
Cut the brown part from the fruit and eat the rest.)
—And so I rested.

Insight often disappears but leaves residue,
what you understand and did not know before.
It is not quite so noisy inside

and then he disappeared.

Narrative: Ali

a poem in twelve rounds

1.

My head so big
they had to pry
me out. I'm sorry
Bird (is what I call
my mother). Cassius
Marcellus Clay,
Muhammad Ali;
you can say
my name in any
language, any
continent: Ali.

2.

Two photographs
of Emmett Till,
born my year,
on my birthday.
One, he's smiling,
happy, and the other one
is after. His mother
did the bold thing,
kept the casket open,
made the thousands look upon
his bulging eyes,
his twisted neck,
her lynched black boy.
I couldn't sleep
for thinking,
Emmett Till.

One day I went
down to the train tracks,
found some iron
shoe-shine rests
and planted them
between the ties
and waited
for a train to come,
and watched the train
derail, and ran,
and after that
I slept at night.

3.

I need to train
around people,
hear them talk,
talk back. I need
to hear the traffic,
see people in
the barbershop,
people getting
shoe shines, talking,
hear them talk,
talk back.

4.

Bottom line: Olympic gold
can't buy a black man
a Louisville hamburger
in nineteen-sixty.

Wasn't even real gold.
I watched the river
drag the ribbon down,
red, white, and blue.

5.

Laying on the bed,
praying for a wife,
in walk Sonji Roi.

Pretty little shape.
Do you like
chop suey?

Can I wash your hair
underneath
that wig?

Lay on the bed,
Girl. Lie
with me.

Shake to the east,
to the north,
south, west—

but remember,
remember, I need
a Muslim wife. So

Quit using lipstick.
Quit your boogaloo.
Cover up your knees

like a Muslim
wife, religion,
religion, a Muslim

wife. Eleven
months with Sonji,
first woman I loved.

6.

There's not
too many days
that pass that I
don't think
of how it started,
but I know
no Great White Hope
can beat
a true black champ.
Jerry Quarry
could have been
a movie star,
a millionaire,
a senator,
a president—
he only had
to do one thing,
is whip me,
but he can't.

7. Dressing-Room Visitor

He opened
up his shirt:
"KKK" cut
in his chest.
He dropped
his trousers:
latticed scars
where testicles
should be. His face
bewildered, frozen,
in the Alabama woods
that night in 1966
when they left him
for dead, his testicles
in a Dixie cup.
You a warning,
they told him,
to smart-mouth,
sassy-acting niggers,
meaning niggers
still alive,
meaning any nigger,
meaning niggers
like me.

8. Training

Unsweetened grapefruit juice
will melt my stomach down.
Don't drive if you can walk,
don't walk if you can run.
I add a mile each day
and run in eight-pound boots.

My knuckles sometimes burst
the glove. I let dead skin
build up, and then I peel it,
let it scar, so I don't bleed
as much. My bones
absorb the shock.

I train in three-minute
spurts, like rounds: three
rounds big bag, three speed
bag, three jump rope, one-
minute breaks,
no more, no less.

Am I too old? Eat only
kosher meat. Eat cabbage,
carrots, beets, and watch
the weight come down:
two-thirty, two-twenty,
two ten, two-oh-nine.

9.

Will I go
like Kid Paret,
a fractured
skull, a ten-day
sleep, dreaming
alligators, pork
chops, saxophones,
slow grinds, funk,
fishbowls, lightbulbs,
bats, typewriters,
tuning forks, funk,
clocks, red rubber
ball, what you see
in that lifetime
knockout minute
on the cusp?
You could be
let go,
you could be
snatched back.

10. Rumble in the Jungle

Ali boma ye,
Ali boma ye,
means kill him, Ali,
which is different
from a whupping
which is what I give,
but I lead them chanting
anyway, *Ali*
boma ye, because
here in Africa
black people fly
planes and run countries.

I'm still making up
for the foolishness
I said when I was
Clay from Louisville,
where I learned Africans
lived naked in straw
huts eating tiger meat,
grunting and grinning,
swinging from vines,
pounding their chests—

I pound my chest but of my own accord.

11.

I said to Joe Frazier,
first thing, get a good house
in case you get crippled
so you and your family
can sleep somewhere. Always
keep one good Cadillac.
And watch how you dress
with that cowboy hat,
pink suits, white shoes—
that's how pimps dress,
or kids, and you a champ,
or wish you were, 'cause
I can whip you in the ring
or whip you in the street.
Now back to clothes,
wear dark clothes, suits,
black suits, like you the best
at what you do, like you
President of the World.
Dress like that.
Put them yellow pants away.
We dinosaurs gotta
look good, gotta sound
good, gotta be good,
the greatest, that's what
I told Joe Frazier,
and he said to me,
we both bad niggers.
We don't do no crawlin'.

12.

They called me "the fistic pariah."

They said I didn't love my country,
called me a race-hater, called me out
of my name, waited for me
to come out on a stretcher, shot at me,
hexed me, cursed me, wished me
all manner of ill will,
told me I was finished.

Here I am,
like the song says,
come and take me,

"The People's Champ,"

myself,
Muhammad.

Neonatology

Is
funky, is
leaky, is
a soggy, bloody crotch, is
sharp jets of breast milk shot straight across the room,
is gaudy, mustard-colored poop, is
postpartum tears that soak the baby's lovely head.

Then everything dries and disappears
Then everything dries and disappears
                              Neonatology

is day into night into day,
light into dark into light, semi-
and full-fledged, hyperconscious,
is funky, is funny: the baby farts,
we laugh. The baby burps, we smile, say "Yes."
The baby poops, his whole body stiffens,
then steam heat floods the pipes.
He slashes his nose with nails we cannot bear to trim,
takes a nap, and the wounds disappear.
The spirit lives in your squirts and coos.
Your noises and fluids are what you do.
                              Neonatology

is what we cannot see: you speak to the birds,
the birds speak back, is solemn,
singing, funky, frightening,
buckets of tears on the baby's lovely head, is

spongy.

"One day you'll forget the baby," Mother says,
"as if he were a pocketbook, a bag of groceries,
something you leave on a kitchen countertop.
I left you once, put on my coat and hat,
remembered my pocketbook, the top and bottom locks,
got all the way to the elevator before I realized.

It only happens once."

We lay on the bed and we rode the gray waves,
apricot juice in a glass in your hand,
single color in this gray light like November.
It is April. We rock.

Then the miracle which is always a miracle happens in many stages,

then the mouth which opens,
the bluebell
that sings.

I was just pregnant,
am no longer pregnant,
see myself in my memory
in overalls, sensible shoes.

Shockingly vital, mammoth giblet,
the second living thing to break free
of my body in fifteen minutes.

The midwife presents it on a platter.
We do not eat, have no Tupperware
to take it home and sanctify a tree.

Instead, we marvel at my cast-off meat,
the almost-pulsing slab, bloody mesa,
what lived moments ago and now has died.

Now I must take the baby to my breast.
There is no mother here but me.
The midwife discards the placenta.

What do you make of this rain, little one,
night rain that your parents have loved all their lives?

From 2 to 3 *The Streets of San Francisco* comes on each night,
and I watch Karl Malden stop crime, and listen

to the mouse-squeak of your suckling, behold your avid jaws,
your black eyes: otter, ocelot,

my whelp, my cub, my seapup.
In the days before you smile at me

or call me Mama or love me,
love is all tit, all wheat-smelling milk, humid crook of the arm

where your warm, damp head seems to live.
I pretend your clasping my finger means you love me.

Dreamt the baby
was born again,
arrived this time in a Moses basket,
had a crone's face,
a Senegalese head wrap,
a pendulous lower lip.

Mamma Zememesh, I dreamt your sister's names.
They floated around me as objects, satellites:

Zayd
      Ntutu
            Yeshareg
                  Asefash
                        Moulounesh

a spinning, turning, turning, spin.

I think the baby needs to eat. The baby's hungry.
Look! He's making sucking noises. Look!
His fist is in his mouth.
Why does the baby sleep all day? How
does the baby sleep at night? Three feedings? Hunh.
90 You need to let that baby cry.
You need to pick that baby up.
You need to put that baby down.
Kiss the baby too much, he'll get heartburn.
What are those bumps on the baby's face?
Why is the baby crying so?
96 That baby needs to eat, and now.

I dream the OB-GYN is here
to spend the night with us. He wears
his white coat and his stethescope
to bed, looks like a loaf
of whole wheat bread. Good-night, we say,
and shut our eyes.
                              The next day
he's up early, jolly. "Time
to have this baby! Tallyho!" And so we do.

All of my aunties chatting like crows on a line,
all of my aunties on electric breast pumps,
the double kind, one for each exhausted tit.

Mommy, the baby's head popped off! A tiny head,
white, wet, bloodless, heartbeat still on the soft spot.
She tells me, Stick it back on, Girl. Don't be afraid.

You can't show your children you're afraid.

A paraffin seam bubbles on his scalp.
A pink cicatrix lines his lovely neck.

Giving birth is like jazz, something from silence,
then all of it. Long, elegant boats,
blood-boiling sunshine, human cargo,
a handmade kite—

                              Postpartum.
No longer a celebrity, pregnant lady, expectant.
It has happened; you are here,
each dram you drain a step away
from flushed and floating, lush and curled.
Now you are the pink one, the movie star.
It has happened. You are here,

and you sing, mewl, holler, peep,
swallow the light and bubble it back,
shine, contain multitudes, gleam. You

are the new one, the movie star,
and birth is like jazz,
from silence and blood, silence
then everything,

jazz.

.

ELIZABETH ALEXANDER was born in New York City and raised in Washington, D.C. She is the author of two previous poetry collections, *Body of Life* and *The Venus Hottentot*. Her poetry and essays have been widely published in magazines, including the *American Poetry Review, Callaloo, Fence,* the *Paris Review, Ploughshares,* and *Poetry,* and in anthologies, including *By Herself: Women Reclaim Poetry; American Poetry: The Next Generation;* and *The Vintage Book of African-American Poetry.* She currently teaches in the Cave Canem Poetry Workshop and at Yale University.

This book was designed by Rachel Holscher. It is set in Janson type by Stanton Publication Services, Inc., and manufactured by Bang Printing on acid-free paper.

Graywolf Press is a not-for-profit, independent press. The books we publish include poetry, literary fiction, and cultural criticism. We are less interested in best-sellers than in talented writers who display a freshness of voice coupled with a distinct vision. We believe these are the very qualities essential to shape a vital and diverse culture.

Thankfully, many of our readers feel the same way. They have shown this through their desire to buy books by Graywolf writers; they have told us this themselves through their e-mail notes and at author events; and they have reinforced their commitment by contributing financial support, in small amounts and in large amounts, and joining the "Friends of Graywolf."

If you enjoyed this book and wish to learn more about Graywolf Press, we invite you to ask your bookseller or librarian about further Graywolf titles; or to contact us for a free catalog; or to visit our award-winning web site that features information about our forthcoming books.

We would also like to invite you to consider joining the hundreds of individuals who are already "Friends of Graywolf" by contributing to our membership program. Individual donations of any size are significant to us: they tell us that you believe that the kind of publishing we do *matters*. Our web site gives you many more details about the benefits you will enjoy as a ìFriend of Graywolfî; but if you do not have online access, we urge you to contact us for a copy of our membership brochure.

www.graywolfpress.org

Graywolf Press
2402 University Avenue, Suite 203
Saint Paul, MN 55114
Phone: (651) 641-0077
Fax: (651) 641-0036
E-mail: wolves@graywolfpress.org

Graywolf Press is dedicated to the creation and promotion of thoughtful and imaginative contemporary literature essential to a vital and diverse culture. For further information, visit us online at: **www.graywolfpress.org.**

Other Graywolf titles you might enjoy are:

Domestic Work by Natasha Trethewey
Tug by G.E. Patterson
Pastoral by Carl Phillips
As for Dream by Saskia Hamilton
By Herself: Women Reclaim Poetry, edited by Molly McQuade